ENTER
MY MIND

SABRINA WATSON

atmosphere press

Dear Reader,

My intention in "Enter My Mind" was to bring awareness to mental health and the struggles people go through every day. I am 24 years old and have been to the bottom and back many times. But just know the journey back is possible. We are not alone, you and I, and there are some amazing people to help. Just push through; the past is gone. No need to waste time looking at it. This book was my journal when I was on a mental health stay away in early 2023. I felt there was nothing left for me and I was struggling with accepting myself. I looked at all the things in the past that I loved and missed. I have around 50 more years to love and miss a whole lot more and right now I have FOMO (Fear of Missing Out). I looked at the future; my hope resides there. This has been my journey on my rollercoaster of life. I'm happy for the people I've met and I am sad for those whom I have lost; for they each gave a part of themselves to me. Rather this be tenderness, torment, love, lust, anger, happiness, or confusion; it's all me. This is what life looks like through my eyes.

This book is dedicated to my strong brother Gavin, my beautiful and funny mother Faydra, my accepting and understanding husband Detavious, my grandma Debi and grandpa Domenick, my grandma Freddie, and all those close to my heart: Gabrielle, Verity, Erum, Jayden, Jonathan, etc.

And especially Nona and Poppy (R.I.P.) for helping me become the person I am today. I miss you so much and will never forget you!

For those I missed, thank you for the support and the push to do it!

Contents

SECTION 5

SECTION 6

SECTION 1

Trinity County

Nowhere in the world compares
The way nature comforts me
An unexplainable feeling
Do not take it for granted
The happiest place on earth
Every summer
My own personal sanctuary
At peace
A summer breeze on my skin
A small hike down a hill
A beautiful crystal creek
Clear enough to swim in
Rush creek runs through the property
Salmon spawning
Carcasses remaining on the rocks
The creek twisting and winding
The massive mountains
Filled with life
Backwoods and interesting places to explore
A surprise with every step you take
Every bird, ant, and bee play their part
Making nature beautiful, magnificent
Sun shining its rays down
Illuminating every shade of color
Pine and oak are not scarce
The most common trees
Supplying clean, fresh air
Filling my lungs
In the fall the leaves change color
Deep orange, red and yellow
Leaves layering the ground

A child playing in a pile
Raking leaves with my great grandfather
Simple little things
Bringing the most joy to me
Piles in the back of a truck
Driving to an open plain
The back of our property
Burning and avoiding the fire
A sense of responsibility
No dad
Grandpa was a role model
Trinity County is like none else
A way of life
Becoming accustomed to
Built me into the woman I am
I'm proud
Nippy, brisk winters
Very gorgeous
Very calm
Big snowflakes
Each one is specially designed
The artist, Mother Nature
Binding together
Forming a blanket
Perfect crochet
If I was lucky enough
Walking the hill to the bus stop
A long driveway
A snowflake would land softly
On my small mitten
I would get to admire it
The delicacy
A beautiful place, my small town

Nona

My words being captured in a recorder
Climbed up on the counter
We had pointless conversations
Growing a little taller
Oranges made for me with oil and pepper
You always wore a turtleneck and sweater, I have one or two now
To remind me of you
Gum wrapper bookmarks
The "crick"
Walking down the hallway
Singing, "I wanna hold your hand"
Sunbathing on the back porch
Driving the explorer, ever so slow
Your goulash we all loved
Scratching Poppy's back
Pouring him a glass of wine
Never drinking because your face turned red
Wanting to get out of the house
To be driven around
Always putting your family first
You would have done anything for us, and you did
I only wish I could have returned the favor
Always letting me know you were there to listen
You got to see me become a young adult
I was crying when I had to say goodbye over video chat
My career choice did not allow me to be there
Oh, the regrets I have
What good does it do now?
Just know I miss and love you
Wherever you may be

Things remind me of you every day
I try not to sob
Your cup of coffee, always going cold
Cuddling with the Idaho potato stuffie
It now remains at home, sitting on my bookshelf
Your bathrobe helps me stay warm
The pink is still so vibrant, though the tie is lost
Been through the wash one too many times
But it remains a blanket of comfort
I read so much now as you did
It was your favorite hobby
Finding comfort in the kitchen's blue chair
Worn with love
Asking me if I'm okay to go out
Are my things in order?
Your windchimes, I can hear them now
I was gifted my own to reminisce
They bring peace
Something I've lacked for such a while
I long to go back to them now
It's been a day too many since you left
Your tuna sandwiches
The crusts cut off
"Diet" everything, low sugar, and prune juice
I know you only cared about my health
Your permed hair, always so white and shiny
Curls puffing out of your head after you slept
Your blue comb and mirror,
I should have sorted that for you
Like you've always done for me

Poppy

The smell of dust in the air
A cool breeze on our skin
On the back of the lawn mower
Grasshoppers hopping up from the grass and weeds
You started a burn pile in our vast backyard
I wanted to partake but I was too young
You were the father figure in my life
My own small fire next to yours
The fire is gone now
But the warmth in my heart still remains
I love you, Poppy
I love the glass of Merlot you requested after dinner
It brings tears to my eyes
The last words you said to me
"I'm proud of you"
When I lost you, the fire flickered but still remains strong
For you, I hope I never disappointed you
Weed-whacking and hard work
We bonded while painting
The sought-after white picket fence
You loved "seetz" scratching your back
In the kitchen, we watched the news
All the football games
I complained but wish I could go back now
You always made sure I put me first
Bluntness, when I wasn't making a wise decision
You cared for me and I miss that
Like when I tried to drive the bug to a boy's house
You had just taught me that day
Of course, I said I was going to a friend's
But you knew well enough

I wish I could reverse time to care for you
I had been selfish
Putting men first that weren't you
Responsibilities lacked
I was a teenager, 18
A Dumbo shirt too big for you
Worn just to make us happy
You provided safety
Paved the way for us to grow
Tagging along to your work, and errands
Everyone knew me because they knew you
Kindness for others radiated in your actions
You did everything you could for your family
How funny you didn't know you were
A bit vulgar, but innocent humor
Sacrifices made against your beliefs
A Christmas tree presented in the kitchen
A "Festival of Lights" in the entry room
Dressing up as bigfoot
You waited with me at the bus stop
Taking me to school if I missed it
You taught me how to make the color green
Mixing blue and yellow highlighters on scrap paper
Sitting on the floor of your office with you
Working away on who knows what
You don't get to see me now
I'm in my 20s
I've grown and become more intelligent
I don't know if I would have left if I knew
Red Solo Cup
That was for me, is for me
Wherever you are now...
I hope I'm still making you proud

SECTION 2

I'm sorry

I don't know what I've done
I left you out to dry
It wasn't my idea of fun
All the weeks passed by, I question why
I was so wrong
You are the blessing I asked for
I've needed you for so long
I shouldn't have opened that door
The one I've pushed you through
You didn't want to go
I felt it was too good to be true
Previous experiences, how was I supposed to know
No matter how badly I treated you
You stayed by my side
I'm feeling blue
Nights I've cried
My mental health got in the way
I loved you then felt nothing
I miss you these days
I'm starting to feel something
I'm sorry
I've got help
My mind isn't so starry
…Well
I welcome you back
Maybe we can try again
Parts of me used to lack
I think of all this as a sin
I understand myself more
My disorders
Time together became a bore

Should have never crossed that border
We were supposed to be married
I let a good one go
Feelings buried
So…
You found me so funny and saw ME
Love has up and downs
I want the bond that used to be
Love has frowns
I needed to focus on myself first
I didn't realize it was this serious
Quench my thirst
I was delirious
Now that the time has come
You don't care to speak
Maybe my idea of a relationship was dumb
I am at my peak
Or so I believe
A refreshed me
What is up your sleeve?
What can I not see?
Are you ready for this?
Am I expecting too much?
I'm clenching my fist
Compared to others you're nonsuch
We've read books together
No more chasing our tail
Birds of a feather
Let this be our fairytale
You're far away
A relaxed brow
I have time to make things our way, I'm ready now

The Bees

It's like bees
Suffocating you
An allergy
On a hot summer day
A buzzing
Tapping of your foot
The Queen, deeply rooted in your chest
The bees go where she goes
You can't breathe
Finally a relief
They flew away
She knows where home is

Solo Part 1

I catch myself calling this hospital home
My safe space to just roam
No judgment, I open up
Everyone can relate and say, "I've been there, I done it"
That means I'm comfortable right?
That I should just sit tight?
But comfort isn't change
Maybe this is an exception
Usually, it's frowned on to stay in a state of acceptation
To push forward you need a sliver of motivation
I can't live my life in isolation
I have become a victim of anxiety, depression, and PTSD
It got to the point where I would say, "Just end me"
A craving for human interaction
How did this happen?
Binge drinking and blacking out
On the street, no sweater, no money
No phone, no shoes, walking about
Dec 31, 2022,
Woke up the next morning, my eyes no longer blue

Solo Part 2

Growing up is supposed to be a time of innocence
Happy times
Times when a family grows stronger
Your bonds are formed
This was fast-forwarded for me
Innocence violated
Learning too much about the bad in life
Childhood wasn't what I imagined
Before having a chance to catch my breath
I was screaming don't leave
Damaged just like me
I was lost
Trying to free ourselves from addictions
Our pain inflictions
Here I am again
Sirens, sedation, airlifts, blood just wondering why
I feel neglected, disrespected, used
When I got that call I would have died for you
Nothing mattered but you
You're the reason I pulled through
Couldn't disappoint you
We never got the childhoods we deserved
Who's to say we can't live it now?
Innocence can still be existent
A new day to get through
Be vulnerable and ask for help
Don't stop yourself
Trust
Trust can be violated
But I would rather deal with that than never trust again

Give me a break
Give myself to someone else
Seek help
Layers of time mixed and mashed
Call me childish if you want
But I won't let what I didn't get as a child be snatched

SECTION 3

Awareness of your Waterfalls

Awareness, to be in this state of mind you cannot be careless
This is the time to think it through and know what you need to do
Sitting by the waterfall, watching all the insects crawl
There are all sorts of specimens interacting with each other now
 and then
We sit by ourselves and observe without speaking a word
Who are we? What are we? What are we for?
What caused life to open this door?
Are the things we see around us normal?
Is there a parallel universe to us more informal?
As I am sitting by my waterfall, the tears fall
Strangers in the street walk by me and don't see a purpose
But we open up and dive under the surface
You can see the past within me
You can see I don't deserve this
No one is better than another at the end of the day
We are all born into different ways
The world is a mess and I'm under duress
Where is the panic button I so dearly need to press
I've found it once
I'm here while I'm speaking
It's been weeks, yet I still lay awake weeping
And waiting for this next stage called change
I don't want to feel how I feel
I want to be me without my painful emotions feeling so real
There's a blockage around me
I don't know what to call it
People think change is as easy as what you pull out of your pocket
I'm trying, I really am
Pointless to me and I don't give a damn

Waiting to be well enough and get back
To a normal life, a happy life, a content life
I'm still working on removing this knife

Bi

A crisp leaf under your foot
A crunch and you just **know** what it is
Surety of your surroundings
Sexuality is confusing
Legal age and still unsure
Do I tell people now or not?
Do I like girls? Do I like boys?
Do I like both?
Everyone can be liked and loved
Who do I see myself marrying?
Being sexually active with?
These are the questions that rattle my brain
Lust, a touch
Bumps on my skin, hair to the heavens
So beautiful
Is this something I need "outside help" figuring out?
Is my questioning enough to know?
I've avoided it long enough
I haven't tried it
Do I need to validate it?
You don't need to announce you are straight
So why is it that when you do the opposite there is hate
Sexuality is not something to feel bad for
We are human
Humans make mistakes
Severe crimes dealt with less judgment
Being gay, bi, trans, fluid, etc. is not a crime
It's who you are, and you have the right

No one can take this from you
You belong in this world
A breath in the cold winter air
A crisp leaf under your foot, you **know** what it is

Live, Die

Live, die, and make the best of it
This life
Document the good and bad
Keep them separated
Look back on it
Reflet
Search for your answers
This is it
Our drive for constant productivity
Lying awake at night
The morning shines in
How many hours passed?
My heart beats in my ears
Oh, how I want to scream
Was this necessary?
This morning air
Will this matter in a week?
No…
Relax
Enjoy the time you got
Do not let others say who you are
Do not let others think searching for answers is wrong
They are not you, don't compare
They do not know you

The War

Bad experiences happen
It can show you who you really are
In your most vulnerable state
Internal strength, focus, and patience tested
For some people, it was a long time
A long time to break
For others, they have been broken their whole lives
Recovering may be harder than what you've been through
It might be the hardest battle yet
When the battle is won
It may be the greatest victory experienced
Winning accompanied by pride
With pride comes confidence
You may surprise yourself with your accomplishments
You may be surprised you broke in the first place
What's most surprising is your honesty
You were able to give yourself acceptance
When the war ends, a celebration begins
You are left a better version of you
A more in-touch version of you
A new meaning of life
A motivation to do the best you can
The time you are fortunate to have
Of course, everything is easier said than done
Or written I suppose
If only life was determined by beautiful words
These words scribbled across paper
Instead, I have bad spelling, and other authors altering my text

SECTION 4

Roadless Journey

It's been a long time coming
A long-time running
Vulnerability is sincere to me
At the ward where I'm meant to be
Patience is what I'm told
But it can be so cold
How much time is enough
Get through it, be tough
I'm crying when I'm woke
I cried when I spoke
Weeping while I sleep
Nightmares and trauma that run so deep
Disorder after disorder
Nothing is in order
Waiting and waiting
Looking for a problem sorter
The battle I'm fighting
It can be so frightening
Affliction after affliction
It seems to be an addiction
Feeling so grim
How do I win?
They say just smile
It's okay
That's how life is?
How can I do that with a heart as cold as ice be?
This masquerade ball cannot be my downfall
Giving the last that I've got
The doubt surrounds me
The Gale is not the destination to be

The space between acceptance and change
It's ongoing
Growing up too fast
Everything was just thrown in
Fastballs are speeding
I've been left bruised and beaten
I'm bleedin'
Find me
Help me, even for a little
I know I'm hard to love
I beg you to not belittle
Never given a road map
I write off the tap
Age 24, kicked through the door
A man betrayed me
I thought I could trust him at the age of 4
Humor and dedication
It's been my medication
To this pain
Every day I wake to the rain
The storm of a new trauma is born
Depression leads to defending
Maybe my life needs ending
My soul leaves
When I go, please plant trees
I want my vibe back
I want my mind back
I call out for motivation
Drive to survive, to thrive
Lost half of myself when my greats died
The other half with attempted suicides
I was a shield for my brother

A shoulder for my mother
Hanging on to the family tree
Grasping with the little of me
Shouldn't be here
Things need to be clear
Sam
I couldn't believe what I heard was true
I got our friendship bracelet
It's still tied around my ankle in place
Like lace
I didn't forget about you
Feeling so hopeless
A life so roadless
Facing what I ran from
Facing this
Please just give me a little somethin'

Enter my Mind

My time is wasting
My heart is surely breaking
I need a fresh start
I need a restart
Everything makes my heart race
Each day is something new to face
Take it in
I never know what to write as a next of kin
Mistreatment, this is indecent
I'm so lost on what I'm meant to be, Pressure to be true
When I enter my mind I always want more
Being authentic isn't something you plan for
My choices have been impulsive
I feel so repulsive
Voices in my mind urging me to get better
Gotta change myself, or this is forever
Loving myself is scary
In my chest, it feels so airy
A feeling of nothing more
I beg to kick down the door
Who am I today?
I need my feelings at bay
No way though
I just want to catch a nonstop train and go
I wear this mask of a joker and a sweetheart
But deep down that's not the only real part
It's exhausting
Being here
With my heart slowly defrosting
Happiness can be so surreal

It isn't something I remember how to feel
I'm scared of what I'm meant to be
The journey to find the missing parts of me
What's it like to know yourself?
To have good mental health?
This mask is coming off
My flaws will shine through
I'm manifesting a sky so blue
A depressed mess
Can you feel this?
Do you really do?
Find your truth
Let you be you

Phobic

When you came in the door
You were so angry with everyone
Coming from you was a roar
What had we done?
I don't think you really meant it
But looks can be deceiving
What you said just didn't sit
We all sat there disbelieving
My friends didn't have to be there
I was upset for them
I stood up with the anger of a bear
I wasn't retreating to my den
People are different than us sometimes
So what?
I gave you a warning, you had time
A knot in my gut
That was something I don't stand for
I didn't want to do it
You fell to the floor
You got hit

Friends Can Break Hearts Too

You're a phony
Someone new came around
You act like I don't exist
Said they have your loyalty now,
What is this?
I bought gifts
They never made it to you
Gifts to someone else
Someone who knew
It suits them better anyway
You used me
My heart, broken
I was pushed away
Good ones now
Worth time
A body of water
I'm swallowed in regret

SECTION 5

Behind the Mask I Wear

Behind the mask I wear
You are unaware
That I also carry a sword and shield
To defend me from those who yield
My armor is very sturdy
Built up throughout my lifetime
This protection is my lifeline
Remove it and I'm exposed and vulnerable
As I present myself to you now
My armor has been removed
But only temporarily
It is being upgraded and repaired
My sword sharpened for those who threaten
Smile you
Don't let them see what you've been through
But do!
Those whose armor is the same as mine
I'm comfortable with
We know what it's like
To carry it every day
My goal is to remove it
Someday entirely around those who are different
Let them admire
Take in and understand
Maybe my differences can help me
It's been hard to see that
I've been scared of them
Perhaps they'll proclaim, "Ew, who is that?"
It's gone better than I thought
I still need work warming up

It's cold out here
But I'm ready to get back into the war
I have my army of soldiers
We stand side by side
They understand me and have helped
Into the battle, we ride

A Day in London

My feet are aching
Pushing through human traffic
My legs are quaking
This is going to make me sick
Man, if another person cuts me off!
Someone bumps into me
I let out a scoff
They were in a rush for their tea
Charity shops were quiet
I scored some new boots
In my head was a riot
Screaming with a hoot
I was with my friends
So good to see them
I don't need to pretend
We are all gems
Shining so freely
It's worth the hustle and bustle
For a few hours of company
I've worked all my muscle
The uncertain rain
Was switched off and on
I wonder if it feels pain
From the street it lands upon
The air was fresh and breezy
But with a lack of sun
The cold nips at me dearly
I'm sure it had fun
For it had been locked away for a while now
It was time to let go

Dancing and coming to a bow
It meant the best, I know it did so
The time come to say goodbye now
We all shared hugs
Meet up on Friday, that was our vow
Freedom was our drug
We had shared meals
We unloaded a ton
All senses touched, it had been so surreal
This was a day in London

A Day in London Part 2

Pimlico, Friday
You two were there waiting for me
I saw your smiling faces
I immediately felt warmth
Warmth after anxiety
A sweaty mess
We are headed to the nail salon!
Lord, I need it
I pick yellow for my fingers
I pick dark grey for my toes
Gotta have a bit of one another
That includes life as well
After that, guess what?
Another charity shop!
I got a classic calf length jacket
As well as some killer Burberry heels
Speaking about killer
That's what almost happened at the Thai food place
If they say something is spicy,
It is definitely SPICY!
Last was the goodbye talk
The goodbye hugs
The goodbye "I'll miss you's"
It's not bye, it's see you later

Books

The smell of a lovingly worn book
Or, one you are lucky enough to be the first to read
Aligned along a shelf like piano keys
Some skipped over
But you retrace
You read the back
Instant regret fills you
You almost dismissed it
Overwhelmed and taken in
You enter a new world
Your world is nonexistent
Everything pushed to the back
Thin pages between fingers
Pride in productiveness
Warmth
Blurry print
A relief spread in your nerves
A chest lightened
Personal emotions locked away
Immersed in a deep sleep

I'm leaving

A bittersweet goodbye
We stand eye to eye
My heart you complete
But my heart skips a beat
I'm excited
Yet frightened
Don't know what to expect
Come save me and direct
I'll miss you
But I need to see this through
Times were enjoyable
What's coming is unavoidable
Stay with me when I leave
I'll keep you up my sleeve
For when I need you, you'll be there
This bond we share

SECTION 6

Perseverance & Safety

Safety is secure
I want to curl up
A padded package
A priceless knick knack
Barriers affect life flow
A river on a fall day
Boulders limiting the natural current
Issues and circumstances
Fish finding their way through
My Personal qualities
Helping to overcome challenges faced
Driftwood to save you and remain afloat
Skills and resources
Supporting and enhancing daily life
Happiness, good qualities, beliefs
The riverbanks
Social, physical, and belief environment
Checkpoints to work through
An un-rounded individual
Uncertainness, family issues, BPD, ADHD
Strength, courage, resilience, independence
Don't worry about what you can't control
Kind, caring, driven, vocal
Open, funny, smart
Therapy, arts, crafts, reading
Supportive friends and coworkers
Light-heartedness and motivation
Hiking, writing, knitting, the place I call home
Free, good health, my irreplaceable cat children
Saving and responsibility

Calm comfort

Looked after tenderness

Perseverance is exhausting

It's about saying no when wanted, yes when needed

Long hours

Faith crushed, though not forever

Grow

Discover your breaking point
Focus on the walk ahead
You've come a long way
The sun, a force for change
Growing, smiling
Creativity running wild
A new way to look
Social circle building
Solutions are coming
See them in the distance
It's what a woman wants!
A touch
Boom, bang
Begin your own tradition
Define your mood
Obliterate guilt
Obliterate anything that stands in your way
Unfold
Potential is our passion
Basic building blocks
Work hard
Work for you
Open the wonder, that is you
Are you prepared to lose all this?
Think about the future
How will it affect you?
A wonderful new development
Undergoing profound change

Carry on dancing
The little things
They matter to the max
Reflect your viewpoint
Your role
Ups and downs
Times of confessions
A gut instinct
Be a rebel
Be human
Be front row
Day by day
All-inclusive
Beautiful and soothing
You won't like it…
But you'll have to
Kind and caring
Warm heart
Through and through
One way or the other
Hit back
Keep fighting
Build purpose
Stand
Find your feet
Access all areas
For all your tomorrows
Offbeat elegance

Vision Board

Objects and destinations we wish to reach
Stuff teachers could never teach
Pasted across a board
To your accord
What do you want out of life?
What do you envision in your eye?
Wind from whispers pushing you forward
A future to look toward
Nails bit down to the cuticle during hurdles
Avoiding re-occurring circles
The work will be worth our control
Do we notice when we meet our goals?
Are we not realizing this before?
Act quick!
Are you always wanting more?
In death, such things serve no purpose
No need to be nervous
It's not wrong to have self-esteem
To have aspirations and dreams
But still, be in the present
Find what lies right in front of you pleasant
Do not hurt your heart, indeed
For things may not succeed
Be grateful for what has
And what you have
Remain hopeful, plan your dishes
Paste your wishes
Manifest what shall come
Determined 101

Home

Urges can be shameful
Intensive talks
You may be moved
Unexpected victories
Alarming mind games
You're ready to do it
For defeats
Crisis for the future you
You found her
Deep in shambles
Deep in pain
Severely depressed
Warm-up
Life imitates art
Does this include tiredness, fatigue, and ill health?
Vulnerable
I needed a kick
Tolerance of the risks
Alarming opportunities
Confidence despite setbacks
Innocence
Build a better tomorrow
Cast your gaze farther
Find and create your home

About Atmosphere Press

Founded in 2015, Atmosphere Press was built on the principles of Honesty, Transparency, Professionalism, Kindness, and Making Your Book Awesome. As an ethical and author-friendly hybrid press, we stay true to that founding mission today.

If you're a reader, enter our giveaway for a free book here:

SCAN TO ENTER
BOOK GIVEAWAY

If you're a writer, submit your manuscript for consideration here:

SCAN TO SUBMIT
MANUSCRIPT

And always feel free to visit Atmosphere Press and our authors online at atmospherepress.com. See you there soon!

About the Author

Sabrina is an independent writer currently residing in Suffolk, United Kingdom. Sabrina was born in 1998 and spent her early years growing up in the Northern town of "Little old Lewiston" in Trinity County, California. When she was 18 she joined the Air Force,

departing from Southern California where she resided during high school.

She holds an Associates degree in Aviation Management and is on the cusp of completing her Bachelor's of Science in Allied Health. She was inspired to pursue this degree after seeing the help healthcare workers provided to those close to her.

Her hobbies involve loving on her 2 cats (Pumpkin and Biggie), thrifting for hidden gems, singing (even if it's just in the comfort of her own home), traveling and unwinding by reading and knitting anything simple! Writing has been a part of her life since the days when her great-grandmother got her published in her hometown's *Trinity Journal* newspaper, a source of immense pride.

Sabrina currently aspires to progress with her career in the Air Force, acquire her dream army green truck and continue traveling the world with her husband and future children.

Join Sabrina on her journey by connecting with her on Facebook, Instagram, or YouTube, where you can follow her adventures and share in her passions: @its__sabrinaa.

Milton Keynes UK
Ingram Content Group UK Ltd.
UKHW012252291123
433483UK00006B/391